# Puzzle Pieces
# that make up a life

Aly Spear

Presentation by *BookLeaf Publishing*

Web: www.bookleafpub.com

E-mail: info@bookleafpub.com


ISBN: 9789357442725

First edition 2024

*For anyone striving to be the best version of themself. Light can't help but come when you live with creativity, hope, and integrity.*

# Dear Reader – See Through New Eyes

I wish you could see yourself through new eyes
get past all those silly little lies
you tell yourself, swearing you need to change
to be worthy, but to me, it all seems strange
I see no pressure to turn your coal into
something shiny
or the way you think your voice sounds whiny
because I already see the diamond you are
never focusing on that one big scar
instead looking at the way you light up a room
and watching your unique brand of magic bloom
seeing how you care so effortlessly
and live in such a magnetic way

so maybe just maybe for one day
you can see yourself through eyes that are not
your own
and learn something you should've always
known
all the beauty you see around and yearn for is in
yourself too
if only you start looking inside of you

# Beginning - The Journey

Maybe it was never about winning
but the true prize was just beginning
by starting you proved them all wrong
even yourself, doubting if you could all along
so remember, the next time you feel fear
your ability to succeed is already clear
for it was always just about trying your best
one step better every day, that is the quest
for if you do that you cannot lose
because it doesn't matter about others' views
you are striving to improve, growing by the
hour
so please never forget your power
and maybe you don't need to have the whole
plan
mapped out and thought through
before you've even began
just start, one moment at a time
and you will climb
the next step will appear
and become clear
if you just keep showing up

# Self-Reflection - The Girl in the Mirror

Do you ever feel a disconnection
to your very own reflection
to the girl in the mirror?
Sometimes I feel like I know her so well
but other times it's hard to tell
the truth of my being
and it feels like a danger
that sometimes I seem like a stranger
even to my very own self
we are enmeshed
yet sometimes we could not be farther apart
so how do I learn to know the depths of my heart
and love every curve

in the way I deserve
when I question if the very essence of my bones
are written in a language
that is almost unknown
all on my own
as I speak in a tongue
long lost to this land
that I don't always even understand
and through that blur
can I see me and her
as one
and drape every part in love?
Undoubtedly so
but before I take that journey, I must know
the innate whispers
and honest musings of my soul
so I can learn to love them all
and accept myself as whole
good and bad like yin and yang
we all bring light but shadows remain
for only with darkness can light shine through
so accepting the shadows is what you must do
and then you can love every single piece of you
looking at your reflection with kindness and care
appreciating every part
that makes you rare
for all the jagged parts make a work of art
like puzzle pieces falling into place
you learn to look at yourself with love and grace

and soon enough you and the girl in the mirror
are one
having accepted every piece of you is what
you've done
feeling whole and complete
because through love, all the parts of you finally
got to meet

# Beauty - Skin DeepER

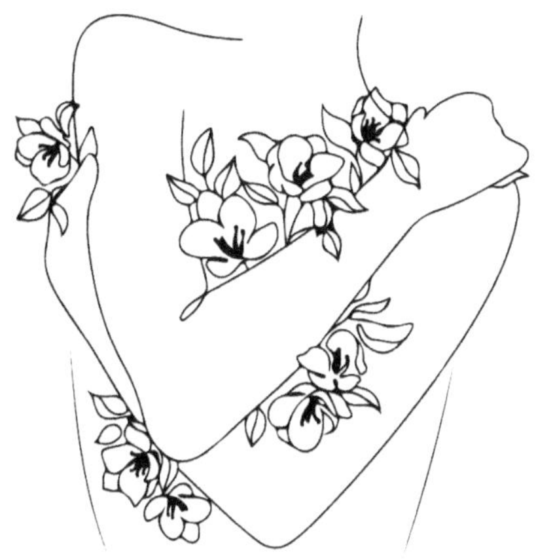

Society often defines beauty
as the curve of her hip
and a touch of her lip
long hair and a booty
blue eyes and a nudie
not the depth of her
or the kindness in her heart
nor that which makes her truly stand apart
not looking at the love she gives
nor the life she lives
an attraction laying purely in the physical
the predictable, the visual
when her deepest beauty
lies in her true essence
her effervescence
in the light she brings

her authenticity, confidence, and in all the things
that make up her beautiful soul
for that, is what truly makes her whole
so if you can look past someone's skin
you might uncover the true beauty deep within

# Career - Finding Your Calling

It's funny how you turn eighteen
wondering, what does life even mean?
But society expects you to have it all figured out
when you barely even know what you're about
so how do you find the career of your dreams
when you've barely even lived, it seems
so much still to grow and learn
clouded by so much concern
so much pressure to earn
because you know you have to provide
but do you even enjoy the ride?
The journey of figuring out your soul's true calling
not just a job, but something truly enthralling

for you see, the most important part
is finding something you can do that lights up
your heart
so don't put too much pressure on figuring
everything out
and thinking there is only one route
give yourself space to breathe and live in the
flow
for when it's right, you will know
and following your dreams
does not have to be as scary as it seems
you can do other things
see what life brings
it can just be taking one step forward a day
and trusting that you will find your way
never silencing the whispers in your soul
but rather listening, and going after what makes
you feel whole

# Childhood Friends - We Will Always Be

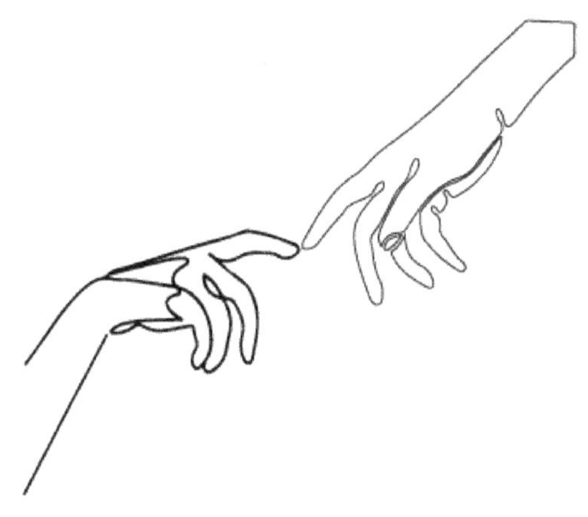

Just because our hands no longer touch
and our voices do not converse much
doesn't mean our bond is no longer
as time goes by, it almost gets stronger
and yes, this love is not what it was
it has transformed because
that is what life does
as we have grown and changed
our lives have rearranged
and we're not those same kids
who stared at the stars
and played on the monkey bars
underneath clouds that danced in the sky
for we have grown apart, you and I

but don't you see
those children we will always be
they live inside of us
even as we live our own day to day
the roots, that foundation, never truly goes away
although the days continue to pass
and we no longer play in the grass
we are grown
on our own, but never alone
because I still live in you
and you in me
for deep down those kids
we will always be

# Toxic ♡ - Adjust Your Crown

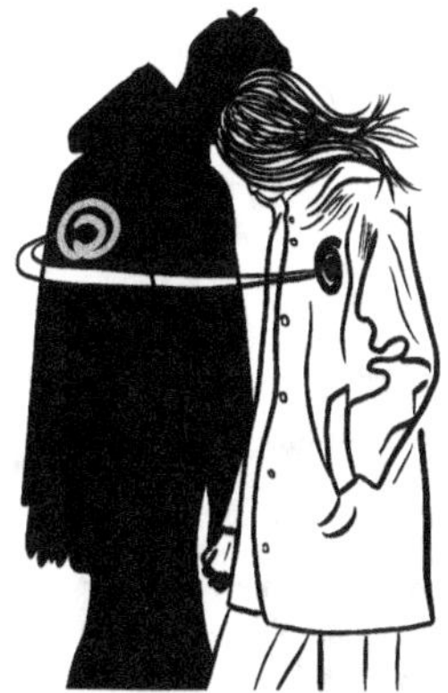

Wipe your tears and adjust your crown
flee the scene before you drown
you were enchanted, opening up the deepest
parts
but ½ truths and manipulation can break two
hearts
so gather your strength and stumble on through
remember the problem was never you
you, my darling, have always been ready
he was the one who felt unsteady
projecting his problems on you
almost like a mirror would do
blaming you as wanting to quit
when he was the very cause of the split
so don't internalize his lies
heal yourself and cut all ties
be fearless as you do
and truly fall in love with you

# Self-Love - What if You Are the Source?

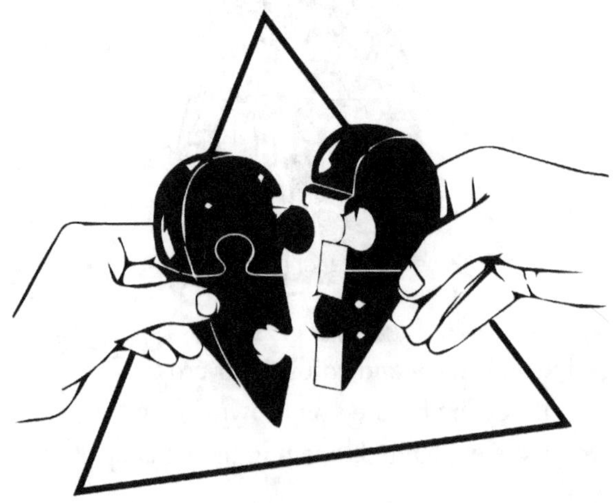

What if you have always been the source
all along the course
of life
and through your strife
did you know you are the one who could give
yourself the love, kindness, compassion and care
you crave
but are you aware
you are also the one capable of taking it all away
when you look at yourself day after day
and speak with spite
that will slowly but steadily dim your own light
so learn to fight
weaving yourself a new tale

choosing strength, self-love, and belief
blazing ahead on your own trail
and promise to speak to yourself kindly
or else you will believe harsh words blindly
rather come home to the truth that love begins
with you
so loving yourself wholly is the only thing to do

# Emotions - Feeling the World

They say mindset is key
and I want to do right by me
striving to always look for the best
and have my positive emotions expressed
but sometimes I cannot control it
my brain throws itself into a fit
surrendering to the chaos locked inside
breaking through all the defenses I've tried
and it is not until I've cried and cried
that I may find the beauty of sweet release
for expressing my emotions brings inner peace
because feeling it all is what lets me truly see
and live a life that is wild, passionate, and free
one where I get to just be me
where the adventures ahead are countless

and joy for life is boundless
listening and hearing the call
while letting myself feel it all
the pain and excitement of growth and
transformation
of creativity, connection, and exploration
balanced out with friendship, warmth, and the
comfort of home
never being lonely, even when alone
with true love, purpose, and fulfillment
a life that is truly brilliant
is out there waiting
for me to be brave enough and get to creating
so today I vow to be authentic and true
to feel every emotion and shine on through

# Heartbreak - Tell Me Why

Tell me why there is no clarity
when two souls split apart
only the silence of a slowly breaking heart
no answers for the unrelenting questions
that set up camp in your brain
and leave behind only pain
swirling around on end in your mind
tell me what truth do you find
in the blurry haze of letting go
do you, like me, question everything you know?
Wondering when the smoke will clear
the fire, all burned out
leaving charred memories and piles of doubt
what destruction lurks in its wake
a choice for you to take
chaos ablaze, the fire also cleanses
giving you the ability to see with new lenses
searching for clarity with no internal clashes
rising up like a phoenix from the ashes

# Moving Forward - Choose You

Don't be so paralyzed with fear
that you stop right here
and don't allow your feet to move forward
don't allow judgment and comparison
to steal your future
focus ahead one step at a time
and be amazed by what you see
when you finally break free
from any confinement you might've placed on
yourself
based on false belief
realizing it was never them
that you alone were the only one
who could condemn
and put limits on your potential
holding yourself back
with all you are

from all you could be
if only you can see that you are strong
and have held the power all along
so all those voices that told you no
it is time to let them go
will you believe their haunted lies?
Or see your life with fresh eyes
and weave yourself a new gorgeous story
choosing strength, self-love and belief
in all its glory
choosing you.

# Hustle Culture - Just Be

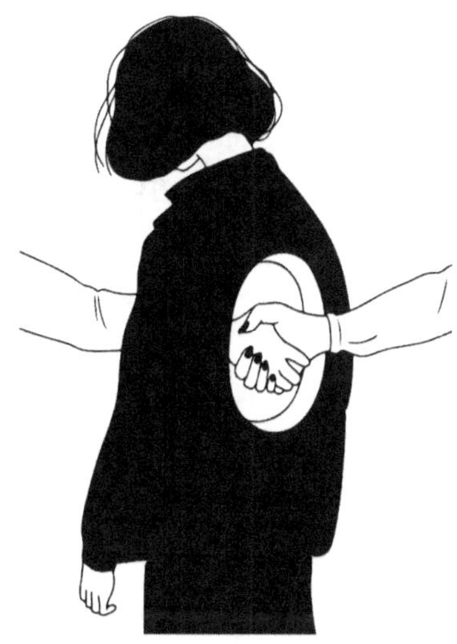

Hustle culture is met with worship and praise
as the only way to be successful
or get a raise
but at the end of the day
can you see past the gray
and the false promise of working your soul away
after all, what happiness can all that money buy
if you have no one to support you when you cry?
Choose work over love enough times
and eventually you will answer for your crimes
all alone
when you should have known
balance was always the key
work hard, play hard,

let yourself rest and just be
and through that mindset
new life can flow
better ideas even and more creativity to show
so maybe just maybe balance you can find
if only you allow yourself to free your mind

# Passion - Flames in the Night

We were like flames in the night
damn, we burned so bright
but when the morning sun rose
and the stars faded away
reality cast a different light
and there's only so long you can fight
to carry the midnights till morning
and intertwine two souls
because you see,
you can't hold the moon in your hand
nor the sun
and love is not something you can demand
or always even fully understand
some paths are not meant to be walked by two
so, as you begin again and bid them adieu
remember that two people sometimes burn so
bright
they're not meant to combine and combust
but rather to be their own light
realizing sometimes space can act like a lighter
and let the two individual souls burn brighter

# Love - Soulmates, the 1

Do you believe in soulmates?
The kind of intertwined love
that starts out unspoken
and cannot be broken
the kind of soul connection
that blazes through
and is always with you
unable to be extinguished
a love so distinguished
selfless, bold, and without fear
a love story that changes and grows but will
never disappear
Raw. Deep. Passionate. Supportive. Honest and
True.
It burns bright too
pushing towards growth, joy and success
while celebrating each other's progress
a partnership that is unifying and grounding
it's almost "too good to be true" sounding
but imagine it is possible that a love like that
does exist
what if it can be yours if you persist?

And choose to love yourself first every day
showing up in your best possible way
so no matter what anyone chooses to say
even if it feels so far away
only accept a love that lights you up
while fully and completely filling your cup
never settling for one that's not true
when deep down you know an epic love is
destined for you

# Connection - Birds of a Feather, Stronger Together

At the end of the day
somewhere along the way
as we search for something more
we forget we're all the same at our core
yet there's so much pressure to have everything
figured out
before we even know what life is truly about
and somewhere along that path
disappointments and anger become wrath
we forget the days when life was play
when we truly connected and lived in the today
now competitions are no longer fun and games
but rather all or nothing for riches and fames
stress, responsibilities, and deadlines added too

tell me, does this sound like you?
But aren't we stronger together?
Like attracts like
like birds of a feather
there's always opportunity
to come together and build community
lifting one another up with every win
for intertwined, we can truly begin
to see that when we are consciously connected
everyone is positively affected

# Awakening - One Life

Awakening, from a long unintended sleep
all these memories for me to keep
as my eyes open wide
I know the universe is on my side
I take this knowledge all in stride
for even with all that I now know
only one step at a time can I go
and as I look, the signs appear
showing me a message clear
each hardship brings a delicate lesson to teach
learning it through growth is always within
reach
you can choose to lean in with grace or fight
with rage

see, what happens next is based on how you
engage
does the pattern repeat?
Or do you learn the lesson
and render the cycle complete
choices always for you to make, or break
this one life to live
how much are you willing to give?
To keep growing higher and higher
and build the life you truly desire
working to make your dreams come true
after all, it's always up to you

# Self-Acceptance - Coming Home

I had to lose who I am, well who I was
to become who I was always meant to be
don't you see?
All the deep pain, loss, transformation, and in
turn joy
was always so much more than a ploy
it was all to come home to the very truth
something I used to know long ago, back in my
youth
that love always began and ended with me
the words I speak
the mindset I adopt
the choices I make
and even weaved into every mistake
all teaching me that the haziest oddities
that make up my beautiful soul

are some of my best commodities
for when you see
your shadows in the same way you look at your
sunniest traits
you set yourself free
accepting every piece with love creates
that safe space
as you realize your true place
and that is when you not only come home to
yourself but realize that yourself was home all
along

# Healing - The Most Beautiful Journey

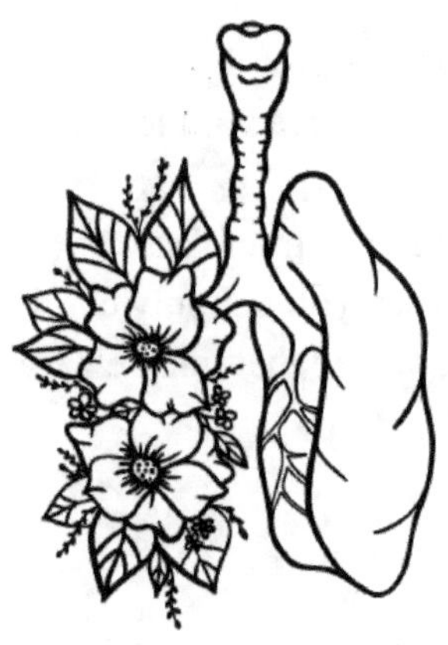

Are you, like me
perplexed and enamored by healing?
It sure brings up a lot of feeling
I used to think it was a destination
but I know that now not to be true
for it is not a place you surpass or stay
but rather, continually move through
it is evolving and ever-present
as the ups and downs of life flow to you
sometimes harsh, other times pleasant
it is one of the constants that does not change
no matter how much knowledge you learn and
exchange
for when it comes to lessons, there will always
be some

for you to navigate and heal from
never will there come a day
when you finally get to say
aha! I am fully healed
as there are always new situations, scars and
triggers to be revealed
living is the only way to truly learn
with love, risk, and striving
that is how you truly start thriving
for healing doesn't always have to be broken
hearts and shards of glass
it can be loving yourself while you wait for the
storm to pass
pouring into yourself in a way you have never
felt
as you tackle problems with which you have
never dealt
using your voice
speaking your truth
as you no longer play a role
but rather come home to your own soul
knowing the most important part
is always checking in with your heart
and when you do that, you can find beauty in
every day
seeing the magic in the adventure along the way
and I think that, perhaps, is the most beautiful
journey of them all

# Life - Work of Art

And I finally saw my life like a work of art
and I started to realize every part
came with lessons so important and true
giving me a perspective I never knew
and while I personally might've liked to have
learned in a different, less painful way
there is a beauty in hindsight, I have to say
like a wave crashing in still water
a chaotic eruption
but with the disruption
comes a new gumption
a fresh burst of energy, a new perspective
that is incredibly effective
at making you question what you thought you
knew

changing your very foundation and life view
so maybe it was a truth you needed to hear
showing you how to break cycles
and making the next step forward clear
no longer are you stuck
so maybe just maybe you turned the chaos into a
strike of luck
and in the end as you heal more and lean into the
flow
that is when you truly know
that everything happened in a way so important
and divine
like pieces of a puzzle that combine
and only by looking back, are you able to see it
all come together beautifully
every part fitting together so suitably
in a way you could've never predicted
your life…truly, a work of art depicted

www.ingramcontent.com/pod-product-compliance
Lightning Source LLC
LaVergne TN
LVHW010940200726
843509LV00013B/2257